EVERY.

SINGLE.

DAY.

Reflections on life, leadership, and love

Joel Morgan

To all of those locked in a cage of their own making—
May you find freedom's key within yourself.

PREFACE

I'm not good at moderation. I don't do "once in awhile" well. For decades, I struggled to exercise some discipline of writing. Nothing worked because I never made a daily commitment. Then, I came across Seth Godin. For well over 6,000 consecutive days, Seth has posted to his blog. His example encouraged me to make the crazy commitment to write and publish something—Every. Single. Day.

What you hold in your hands is the selected results of the first year of my daily Reflections (joelmorgan.com/reflections). It is not meant to be read straight through, but more like a devotional or break time injection of (what I hope is) insight and inspiration.

While I write and publish every day, I had not planned to curate and then publish these writings in book form. Then, Pam, a client (and now friend) of mine kept telling me, "You *have* to publish these!" So with the extra encouragement of my family, Jennifer, Noah and Adam; my friend and awesome author Valley Haggard; and the expertise of layout and design guru Rob Collins; *Every. Single. Day.* was birthed.

I hope these writings cause something powerful to well up inside of you and break forth to change your world.

RE-CREATE

When you do something
every day,
it becomes part of who you are.

So if you,
curse yourself,
pity yourself,
tell yourself you'll never be loved;
if you
eat too much,
drink too much,
sleep too little,
move too little,
you begin to think this is your life.

It's true only if you let it be.

If you dedicate yourself
to something different,
some small change,
every day.

Every.
Single.
Day.

You become someone different.
You begin to re-create yourself
one day at a time.

LEARNING TO LIVE

Saying "I am enough"
doesn't mean you stopped striving.
Having compassion for yourself
doesn't mean you're soft.
Tending your life
doesn't mean you're self-centered.

It means you're learning to live.

DISCIPLINE

Learn this:
discipline is freedom
not bondage.
Set your routines, your rituals
towards Life
and be free.

WHICH PATH?

Which path will you choose today?
The path of darkness
or
light?

Both are always available.

THE PROJECT OF LOVE

Apply yourself,
long term,
to the project
of love.

WHEN DID THE RUT BECOME THE HORIZON?

One day the edge of our rut became the
horizon.
Not all at once, or else we would have
noticed.

Once, we saw all the options, the openings,
the possibilities.
Then,
we settled,
we compromised,
and the rut got deeper.
Our vision grew smaller.
The possibilities fewer.
We accepted what others said:
Too old,
too young,
don't have the right letters after your name.
Too fat,
too skinny,
too short,

too tall,
too ugly,
too whatever
We got comfortable there.
The rut grew deeper.

The rut is a lie we tell ourselves.
There is an entire world beyond the edge.
We have the opportunity to see it
when we stop and ask
how we got this deep.

DEFINITION

Once you have the degree,
the first job,
the promotion,
the pay raise,
the apartment,
the new car,
paid off the debt;
at every point you'll be asking
"What's Next?"

You must define what success is
for YOU.
Not what your mom,
or your lover,
or your industry,
or the culture,
thinks.

When you craft your definition of success
What's Next is no longer a question.

FULFILLMENT

What keeps us from fulfillment?

A decision we made long ago,
which served us then, but gave us:
fear,
shame,
doubt,
worry,
now.

As the saying goes,
"What got you where you are
won't take you where
you need to go."

Make a new decision.

THANK YOU

Two simple words.
What your mother taught you to say.
But we forget.

Everyone benefits from hearing these two
words—sincerely offered.
The barista, the checkout person,
our co-workers, our family members.
Say it to yourself.
More often.

Say Thank You.
Change your world.

MORE THAN JUST NOT GOING TO WORK

When was the last time you planned your
day off?

When was the last time you didn't let
the soccer games,
the yard work,
the random feeling of obligation,
the temptation of "doing nothing,"
run over a day filled with possibility?

What if, on Monday,
you planned your Saturday
and had something more to look forward to
then just not going to work?

SEEK SHELTER

Seek shelter,
but not to hide

Too often the "safe places" we create
become our prison:
the medications,
the anxiety,
the alcohol,
the overeating,
the "I'm so busy,"
the depression,
the labels (which become our identity),
lock us up.
It's not shelter, it's hiding.

So come out.
Seek shelter,
create structure,
routines,
rituals.
Create a container on which to stand
and be opened up to the life
waiting for you,

when you quit hiding.

Seek shelter.

THE HARD WORK OF HAPPINESS

The gurus make it sound easy,
effortless,
instantaneous.

"Just wake up happy," they say.

I say, "Do the hard work of happiness."
Train your brain,
condition you emotions,
move your body,
focus your attention.
Every. Single. Day.

Do the work
and you might just get past fleeting
happiness
and find joy waiting for you.

INVISIBLE BARS

We lock ourselves in cells with
invisible bars.
No one can see them,
but we feel them.

We think they keep us safe,
from ourselves,
from others,
from worry,
from fear,
from shame.

They do keep us safe,
from wonder,
from joy,
from mercy,
from grace.

After a while, we get used to them—
like a baby elephant gets used to being tied
up with a certain length of rope—
forgetting we have the key to set ourselves
free.

What keeps you in your invisible cage?
When will you set yourself free?

LOST IN TRANSITION

The way forward looks different
uncharted,
untested,
unstable.

The landmarks are unfamiliar.

You feel anxious,
frustrated,
and unsettled.

Lost in transition.

Our tendency would be to curl up,
stay stuck, and follow the fear of
unknowing.

But, this is the time to be curious.

You're about to have a breakthrough,
a new discovery,
the path is about to open up,
if you will.

TODAY IS YOUR SOMEDAY

Too many of our hopes,
our dreams,
our ideas
die
under the heading of "Someday."

Isn't today Someday?
Isn't now as good a time as any?

Why not have a bias for action:
Make a decision,
do something,
even if it ends up being wrong.
The more decisions you make,
the better chance you have of getting it
right.

Your Someday is Today.

GET IT WRONG

Everything about our education,
our working world,
our religions,
seem to be about "getting it right."

Don't mess up or you'll get zapped.
Getting zapped is life-ending, catastrophic.
"This will go on your permanent record."

What if it's really about getting it wrong?
About making a mess, cleaning it up
and learning in the process.

What if we could relearn?
What if when we got it right the first time,
we worried that we hadn't really done the
work?
And we took apart the "right answer" to
find all of the wrong ones it contained?

Free yourself to get it wrong,
and you'll be getting it right.

BE THE HERO

Begin by asking:
Who will I be the hero for today?

My lover?
My kids?
My neighbor?
My boss?
My co-workers?
My community?
My school?

Myself?

Today is the day to start being the hero.

INSTEAD

Why not assume the best
instead of the worst?

Why not question your perspective
instead of taking it for granted?

Why not look to give
instead of expecting to get?

What do you need to do "instead"?

I'VE BEEN PREPARING FOR YOUR ARRIVAL

What did you do this morning?

Hit snooze,
roll over,
pull the pillow over your head,
curse the sun,
and begin dreading the events not yet
occurring?

What if?
You set your morning routines and rituals
to move your mind
to positive,
to open,
to curious,
to grateful.

Then, let the events not yet occurring, begin
to occur
and greet them:

"Good Morning, I'm pleased to meet you. I've been preparing for your arrival."

CHOOSE

The power of choice is
an unwelcome truth.

We like to think we are "caught" in bad
situations,
emotions,
relationships,
and we cannot get out.

Truth: We choose to stay caught
through our daily
thoughts,
rituals,
routines,
habits,
comfort.

Truth: The way out is a choice.

Choose.
Take responsibility.
Act.

(rinse and repeat until you are free)

Will you stay caught or will you choose a new way?

COMPASSION

"suffering alongside of"
We are often good at giving others a little
"slack"—
offering Outward Compassion

We are practiced in not giving ourselves the
same.
We block Inward Compassion,
fearing it leads into the mire of self-pity.

The problem: You cannot give what you
do not have.

So if you don't have Inward Compassion,
what is it you are giving to others?

RELATIONSHIP CUSTOMER SERVICE

On a scale of 1 to 10, how is our
relationship this week?
If it's not a 10, what needs to happen to
make it a 10?

Be willing to ask the question,
receive the answer,
and open yourself to growth.

A more loving,
passionate,
and playful relationship
is two questions away.

MY PLEASURE

Servers at restaurants often say,
"No problem."
when I say, "Thank You."

Then, one day, a server said,
"My pleasure."
and meant it.

What if
loving,
helping,
serving others
was our pleasure,
not a problem?

MULTIPLICATION

We live with the lie of scarcity.
"There is not enough to go around."
Not enough
money,
food,
shelter.

So we scramble,
gather,
hoard,
invest,
always thinking it's not enough.

When we believe this lie,
resources become even more
disproportionately distributed.

What if we believed there was enough—
enough resources
and enough
love,
mercy,
grace,

for everyone to flourish?

When we give, serve, love, contribute,
it's not subtraction.
It's multiplication.

BE KIND

"Be kind. For everyone you meet
is fighting a battle you know nothing
about." —*source unknown*

For years I tried to
drown myself,
kill myself,
because I believed no one in the whole
world
was struggling like me.

Everyone else looked perfect.

Oscar night, red carpet,
tux and elegant gowns—
Perfect.
Flawless skin, six-pack abs, square-jaw,
happy faces—
Perfect.

It was a lie.
And I believed that lie more than I believed
in God.

I don't remember exactly when I saw the truth.

Now I see people.
People who have experienced
amazing things,
troubling things.

Alcoholics and addicts,
recovering,
who embody such beauty.

Outsiders who wonder if they will ever fit in.
Insiders who fear they will fall from grace.

The depressed and anxious,
hoping to be set free.

And those who continue to believe their struggle
is not shared
by anyone else.

Everyday I remind myself:
that the red carpet is not what it seems,

that the lift, the tuck, the practiced smile
often covers what is real,
that we must all learn
through difficulty,
through pain—real or imagined,
if we are going to become real ourselves.

The time this takes is unknown.

For each person has their own
hero's journey
(as corny as that sounds).

When we discover we are the hero,
we begin to see how the struggle,
the dark night,
the days we shouldn't have lived,
fit.

And then, we learn to be kind.

HOLDING ON

"You can't sing."
"You don't write well."
"Our family isn't athletic."
"You'll never make it as an artist."

Something a teacher told us,
Something a parent said,
Something a random stranger pointed out—

we decided to hold on to it,
to incorporate it into our identity.

Maybe it was the way your mother cleaned
the house,
the way your father mixed a drink
every night,
the expectation of perfection,
or being told to hide who you were.

True or not,
real or imagined
holding on to it may or may not be helpful.

SEE IT AS IT IS

Adjust your perspective.
See everything as it is—

No better
No worse

This may take some doing.
Our perspectives are limited
by our attachments,
our emotions,
our blind spots.

You may need help:
from a friend,
a coach,
a therapist,
an accountant,
a doctor,
a lawyer.

Whatever it takes,
Adjust your perspective.

Once you know everything as it is,
You can decide where you want to be.

SHIFT THE WANTING

I used to want to be someone else.
smarter,
stronger,
successful.

I lusted after other's lives.
I lived vicariously,
and felt empty.

Then, I began to see behind the curtain.
What I thought was success often hid
broken relationships, selfishness, and
unhappiness.

So I took a new look inside.
I wanted to see what it was like to be...me.

I began to imagine myself—
10 years in the future.

I asked,
"What does he do?"
"What does he care about?"

"How does he show love?"
"What does he feel like every day?"
"What is his reason for living and loving?"

I shifted the wanting,
and started
becoming.

WHAT ROLE DO YOU PLAY?

When you review the story of your life, what role have you been playing?

Warrior?
Villain?
Joker?
Lover?
Sage?
Saboteur?
Hero?

You're writing the story, so choose your role.

TRUST YOURSELF

Maybe it was the first time
I spoke my truth
and
didn't give credence to the dark voice inside
my head saying,
"Be quiet or they won't like you."

Trust Yourself

Maybe it was after years of keeping
small promises
to myself.

Trust Yourself

Maybe it was when I embraced the idea of
everyone being
worthy of love
and
extended it to myself.

Trust Yourself

What it means:
I am free to speak my truth
and
open a space for others to speak theirs;

I am free to assess my actions,
and see them for what they are;

I am free to pursue my dreams,
not someone else's.

Trust Yourself

Even when the world,
your mother,
your lover,
or
your own dark voice
says otherwise.

Trust Yourself

Will You?

FORGIVE

Yourself.

Yes.
Forgive yourself.

For the mistakes,
missed opportunities,
wasted time.

Holding on to this hurt.
is holding you back.

The way forward cannot
be forged while you are tied to the past.

It's time.

Forgive.

BEGIN AGAIN

Every new day,
when the earth has taken its turn around
the sun,
after we have awakened from our evening
slumber,
our body,
our mind,
our spirit,
tells us there is new possibility.

Since a day has passed,
we are older,
more experienced
(wiser?).

And today,
we have the opportunity
to
begin again.

We can use all of
the experience,
the wisdom,

the knowledge,
the triumphs,
the heartbreaks,
and engage the possibilities,

or not.

The offer stands,
every time the earth moves around the sun.

Begin.

ONE DAY

One day, I'll ask for a raise.
One day, I'll quit and follow my dreams.

One day, I'll get sober.
One day, I'll go to the gym.

One day, I'll tell them how much I love
them.

One day, I'll ask for forgiveness.
One day, I'll forgive myself.

One day, I'll trust myself.
One day, I'll love myself.

One day, I'll be happy.

One day…

UNBROKEN

Breaking free has the word, "break" in it.

You will need to break through your fears.

Then, you will break
your old rules,
your thought patterns,
your work patterns,
your unhelpful habits.

You will practice
taking a break,
to listen to the birds,
smell the fresh cut grass,
and still the turbulent waters of your mind.

And when you have broken everything
unhelpful,
unforgiving,
and unloving—

You will find yourself
unbroken.

ASK FOR WHAT YOU WANT

We are taught
to put ourselves last,
to make sure everyone else
gets what they want first.

It's a wonderful way to remind us to think
of others,
to care for others.

The dark side is when we take it too far,
and never speak for ourselves,
never ask for what we want
and secretly wonder why we are
angry and unsatisfied.

Aren't we doing what we were taught?
Isn't it supposed to bring us joy?

Asking for what you want does not mean
others don't get what they want or need.

It means you are paying attention to

your needs,
your desires,
and
when you ask for what you want,
you give permission for others to do the
same.

Today, ask for what you want.

BABIES

When a baby comes into a room,
don't look at them,
look at the reaction of those around you.

Eyes brighten,
smiles form,
moods change,
hearts soften and open in welcome.

Imagine if this happened whenever
anyone
came into our presence.

What if you treated everyone like a special
gift—
welcoming everyone with joy and
openness?

We were all babies, once upon a time.

WORTH IT

Saying, "I'm good enough"
gets laughs on Saturday Night Live.

Saying, "I'm good enough"
isn't encouraged.

We are told it's silly, selfish, and self-
centered.

Maybe we should change it to:
"I'm worth it".

I'm worth
the time to care for my body,
mind,
spirit.

I'm worthy of the
love,
grace,
and forgiveness
I give to myself.

Cultivating your worth
means you have more to give.

It's not selfish.

When you have more to give,
others feel worth it, too.

You're worth it.

GUT IT OUT

We clench our teeth and push harder.

We think it will make us stronger.

In many cases, it just makes the problem
last longer.

With the clench and push,
we stuff everything down.

We think it's hidden away,
packed and sealed for the rest of our days.

Over time,
the container can no longer hold
and then we explode.

There is a time to push through,
to use our will to make a way.
There is also a time to get help,
a partner, a therapist, a coach.

And like most things, earlier is better

than later.

Are you just gutting it out?

ONE THING

Imagine you triple-booked an appointment,
and all three people showed up.

You decide to meet with them.

There is cross-talk, talking over,
talking through,
and lots of, "What did you say?"

All of them thank you for the time,
and leave unsatisfied,
while you are left to wonder:

what. just. happened?

We do this everyday.
We keep standing appointments with
Email, Facebook, Instagram, Text...

And at the end of the day we wonder:
what. just. happened?

Focus on one thing at a time.

Discipline your mind.

DO IT NOW

Whatever you have been thinking about
to change your day,
to change your work,
to make the world better.

Do it now.

Nothing changes by thinking about it.

DON'T WAIT

To love yourself
To introduce yourself
To ask her out
To tell him you love him
To walk out
To start over
To live your purpose
To serve others
To bless others
To start your business
To quit complaining
To ask for assistance
To be in the moment
To act

What are you waiting for?

SHOW UP

Today,
commit to showing up.

Don't hide.

Take (what feels like)
the risk to be
real,
authentic,
vulnerable.

We are all waiting for
You.

MIND THE GAP

Traversing the gap between
where you
are
and where you want
to be
is a courageous journey.

The path is not clearly marked.
The turns have not been identified.

So, after naming the gap,
determining the destination,
and taking the first step,
you must keep
walking,
falling,
and
getting up—
over and over.

It's going to be
uncomfortable,
awkward,

and painful.

Mind the gap
and
focus
on the destination.

IN THE GAP

Pay attention to where you are.

You are in the gap--
on the journey
from
where you are
to
where you want to be.

In the gap,
you can see where you have come from—
how many steps are behind you—
and celebrate.

You can also see where you are going,
and anticipate the next step.

Don't let the distance to your destination
take you away from this moment
or
make you hesitate to move forward.

In the gap,

pay attention to where you are.

Our lives are spent in the gap.

JUMP THE GAP

Regularly see yourself
reaching your destination,
crossing the finish line,
being the person
you are seeking
to become.

See it.
Feel it.
Taste it.
Touch it.
Smell it.

Jump the gap
from where you are
to
where you want to be.

The more real your destination is to you
now,
the more likely it becomes real
later.

Take time every day
and
jump the gap.

VALLEY IN THE GAP

When traversing the gap—
the path between where you are
and where you want to be—
you will find yourself in
a valley.

The destination will look
farther away than ever.
The next step will take more effort.
You will be tempted to set up camp.
Going back will also look like a good
option.

Keep walking.

(Warning: There are probably more valleys
ahead.)

DISORIENTATION

Once you've taken steps toward your
destination,
you may experience some disorientation.
The old you is clamoring to stop,
to turn around,
to go back
to comfort,
to familiarity.

The new you is still an infant
overshadowed in an instant,
by the confusion,
the disruption,
the new path being trod.

Your first inclination may be to give up
or to push harder forward.

Be still,
feel the confusion,
the disorientation,
the frustration,
and know—

This is the way of transformation.

THAT YOU ARE EVEN ALIVE

There is a time
to stop,
to think,
to realize
and be in wonder
that you are even alive.

The billions of
biological,
geological,
astrological,
historical,
circumstantial,
pieces perfectly put together
to equal

you. here. now.

Mindblowing.
World-changing.

There is a time to be in wonder,

to take hold of the unique opportunity
that you are even alive.

That time is always now.

MAKE A MASTERPIECE

Ask yourself,
"What am I creating?"

A healthy body?
A fulfilled life?
A passionate relationship?
Or
A tired body?
A stress-filled life?
A roommate?

You are the
master craftsman
of your own life.

Make a masterpiece.

TELL BETTER STORIES

We create stories for every situation.

"She's out to get me."
"He just doesn't care anymore."
"I'm beyond help."

In our mind, the story becomes
powerful,
persuasive,
personal,
real.

"I'll never survive this."
"I cannot bear it."
"I'm all alone."

We rehearse these stories as if
there were no other way to tell them.

We forget:
We are the storytellers.

Tell better stories.

ACCEPTANCE

When you finally accept what is
you can imagine what is
Next.

MAMA SAID

Mama said
there would be days like this;
when the twisted story of
anger
and
hurt

overwhelms

the better story of
patience
and
care.

On days like this,
seek silence,
gentleness,
kindness—
for yourself
and for all.

For on days like this,
the twisted story

ties everyone up
in knots
which are not easily undone.

WE BUILD THESE WALLS

With an intention of protection,
we build these walls.

After hurt,
pain,
shame,
we lay another brick.

In the beginning,
the wall serves a good purpose,
keeps us safe.

Later, we realize
what we constructed to protect us
now holds us,
confines us,
imprisons us.

What we have built,
must be undone.

So we say

"Thank you for your protection;
Thanks for keeping me safe;
It's time you served a different purpose."

Then, we begin removing bricks
to open a door
to freedom,
to love,
to abundant, unrestricted life.

The walls we built
become the entryway
to a new tomorrow.

OTHER VOICES

Other voices
sound so eloquent.
Other writers
find words of beauty.
Other bodies
look so fit and strong.
Other lives
seem more fulfilling.

Why is our perception so skewed
in favor of anyone other than ourselves?

When we begin to value our voice,
write our words,
befriend our bodies
without the dark veil of devaluation;

When we begin to accept
and
challenge ourselves to be better
every day;

This is when our life begins

and the other becomes
just an-other on the journey.

DO ONE THING

When you're
overwhelmed,
swamped,
buried,
inundated
and tempted to be paralyzed,

do one thing.

JUDGE

A judge sits on the bench of our mind;
a tyrant, with a Napoleon complex,
weighing in on every
thought, sight and sound.

"Nice hair"
"Did she look in the mirror before she left
the house?"
"What were you thinking"
"They are all
smarter,
better looking,
more successful,
(fill in the blank with something negative)
than you."

Every moment of every day,
court is in session.
We think we are the only ones on trial.

The unspoken truth:
Everyone has their own courtroom.

So while each of our lives is unique,
our journey peculiar,
we all face the judge.

And when we do,
we realize we are hearing our own voice;
we judge ourselves.

The question is:
What will you do with the judge?

DON'T THINK

Set your days
so the
most important tasks
require little willpower.

Put out your workout clothes.
Throw out your kryptonite foods.
Have your journal and pen at the ready.

Schedule your
workouts,
meditation,
prayer,
writing,
relationship time
as you would a meeting with the CEO.

Give your mind a break
so it doesn't have to think.

STUCK IN TRANSITION

When you're in between
one thing and another,
one way of life and another,
one decision and another,
you can get stuck.

Whether it's
between single and married,
between school and full-time work,
between work and retirement
or some other

in between,

transitions are opportunities
for our fears to freeze us.

Transitions are also time
for creativity,
for imagination,
for breaking free.

When in transition,
will you choose
frozen
or
Free?

WHEN IT ALL FALLS APART

You get to see what you are made of.

DECIDE AND DO

Nothing happens until you decide.

When you hesitate,
someone else,
time,
or circumstance
makes the decision.

Once you decide,
you must act
or the decision means little.

Decide and do. (repeat)

EXPRESSION

Depression
mutes
expression
and asks us
to pay
attention.

Be curious.

Investigate.

You may find
a new way
when the path
seems darkest.

THE UNKNOWN

You've been here before,
even if your mind tells you differently.

Once,
eating,
walking,
talking,
were unknown to you.

You learned.

You faced the unknown.

Today,
you may be in-between,
unsure about what comes next
and how to create the life ahead of you.

Don't let the unknown stop you.

Remember, you've been here before.

HABITS NOT INTENTIONS

We walk on the path of
"I should…"
"I could…"
and these
Intentions
become mile markers
on the way to
no
where.

Habits,
chosen and formed with care,
propel us forward with
purpose
and
power.

Habits not intentions.

THAT KNOT IN YOUR STOMACH

You know,
that knot in your stomach,
the one telling you:

"You will fail."
"Don't risk it."
"No."

It's only right if you
don't take the next step.

Let that knot in your stomach
untie itself.

Say:

"Failure is learning."
"I'm in!"
"Yes"

Then, take the next step.

THOSE DAYS

We all have
those days—

tired,
uninspired,
pull the covers back over your head
days.

They can be
a blip
or an SOS.

If they come every once in awhile,
we trust our routines and rituals
to pull us forward.

If they come in bunches,
pay attention.
Discover the message you are being sent.

ENDINGS

Days end.
Nights end.
Weeks end.
Months end.
Years end.

We take this as it is.
We trust this is
simply what happens,
and move forward.

Relationships end.
Jobs end.
Life ends.

We don't often take these as they are.
We don't trust this is simply what happens.

What if we
honored,
mourned,
celebrated,
all these endings

and then
simply,
powerfully,
gracefully,
moved forward?

DISCIPLINE VERSUS REGRET

A doctor recently said to my son:
"There is discipline and there is regret.
Today, I have to work 12 hours. It's a long
day.
Today, I will treat people who have trouble
getting out of a chair.
They regret that they didn't take better care
of their bodies.

So today, I got up at 4:45 am to work out.
That's discipline.
I did it so when I am older, I can still get
out of a chair,
and don't regret that I didn't take care of
my body.
You can choose discipline or regret."

Today, which will you choose—
discipline
or
regret?

PULL OR PUSH?

"You have to push yourself."
How many times have you heard or
thought this?

Do you find life better when someone is
pushing you?

When pushed, our tendency is
to resist,
to push back.

Or would you rather be pulled forward,
beckoned into a life of meaning,
purpose and fulfillment?

When we create a compelling future,
it draws us forward.
We become eager to take the next step(s).
We see the goal and the path becomes
clearer.

SILENCE

Accept the gift of silence.
Nurture the ability to quiet
your heart, mind, and spirit.
Let silence respond first to every question.
Then, you may find your answers.

THE ELEPHANT IN YOUR MIND

The thing you want to ignore.
The obsession.
The addiction.
The hurt.
The guilt.
The anger.

The more you try to ignore it,
the larger it grows.
Just like when someone says,
"Don't think of an elephant."

So I say:
Think of the elephant, give it a name
and deal with it.
They are easier to train when they're small.

WORK HARD,
DO GOOD WORK

Every day, I say to my kids,
"Work hard. Do good work."

Saying this reminds me to do the same.

Work hard:
Get up early.
Get enough rest.
Exercise.
Eat good food.
Do due diligence.
Never stop learning.

Do good work:
Spend time developing relationships.
Respect others.
Serve others.
Make a contribution.

Sometimes I get it right.
Sometimes I don't.
But every day,

I encourage myself:

Work hard. Do good work.

UNEXPECTED

What if you met
anger with acceptance,
frustration with forgiveness,
brokenness with balm,
petulance with patience,
wariness with welcome,
fear with fortitude?

Do the unexpected.

SEED CORN

Kernels grow where they are planted,
never doubting they were supposed
change,
transform,
and produce their fruit.

They don't seem to
wonder
if they should have been a
sunflower,
or a stalk of wheat.
They don't hold on to the seed
and resist
sending down roots,
sending up a stalk.

There are seeds in us.

Will you let them
grow,
transform
and produce your fruit
or are you holding on to the seed?

The world is waiting to enjoy the harvest.

SELF CONFIDENCE

Self confidence
is built
by
keeping promises
to
yourself.

OUT THE DOOR

There are days
where simply getting
out the door
is a triumph.

Much of life is found in
showing up,
so if it takes everything you've got
to be physically present—
do it.

However, when you've given
everything
simply to show up,
you don't have much left to
contribute.

You're there,
but not really.

If weeks and months pass
just getting out the door,
you're existing,

not living.

Don't let your life be just
trying to get out the door.

THE BULLY

When was the last time
you stood up to
the bully
in your life?

The one telling you
(despite all of your
gifts,
skills,
accomplishments)
"You're no good,"
"You're ugly,"
"You'll never amount to anything,"
"You might as well give up."

The problem is, for most of us,
the bullies in our lives
don't live down the street,
or around the corner,
they live in our minds.

And we must learn
how to overcome

our greatest opponent,
ourselves.

YOUR TRUE SELF

"I'm not feeling like myself today."

We have this sense that there is an "us,"
a true self,
just out of our reach.

We are right:
We all have a true and best self,
and if it's out of our reach, we have put it
there.

Our fears,
our insecurities,
our habitual emotional responses
keep us from living what we know is true.

Still, there are
bright spots—
these moments and days,
when we get out of our heads
and into our hearts,
to act, speak, and love as our true self.

Living your Life
is nurturing those bright spots,
to name, claim, and live
our true self
every
day.

May you feel like your true self today.

WHACK-A-MOLE

Did you ever play Whack-A-Mole?
You get a mallet, and every time a mole
pops out of a hole, you try to whack it.

We play whack-a-mole by
paying attention to whatever pops up:
emails,
texts,
likes,
ding,
buzz,
chirp.

By giving everything attention,
we pay real attention to nothing.

Whack-A-Mole is a fun game,
but no way to live your life.

CONSPIRE OR INSPIRE

"Who killed JFK?"
"One world government."
"The moon landing."
All conspiracy theories have something in
common.
They are born out of fear.

Fear conspires.
It sees connections,
evil intentions,
and dark associations.

Faith inspires.

Faith sees opportunities,
assumes positive intent,
and seeks connection.

Fear conspires.
Faith inspires.

GO FIRST

Everyone wants to be first,
#1,
the Gold Medalist.

However,
no one likes to go first--
for fear of looking stupid,
making a mistake,
being a "teacher's pet."

If we're going to do work that matters,
we're going to have to
raise our hands,
step up,
and pick ourselves.

Today, why not go first?

LEARNING DAY

You need days
to soak in something new,
to hear a different voice,
to be challenged.

You need time
to listen,
to ponder,
to sit in wonder.

This is learning day.
(When was the last time you planned one?)

DECISION DAY

The day when you
draw a line in the sand,
when you say, "This changes NOW!"
when you declare, "No more."

The day when something you
"should" do becomes "must" do
and life will never be the same.

This is decision day.
(What do you need to decide?)

EMBRACE FEAR

All the gurus and motivators say it,
but what does it mean to "Embrace Fear"?

I think it means acknowledging the
voice(s) in our head that says,
"It's too risky."
"It's too difficult."
"People will think you are weird."
and moving forward anyway.

Some of the most amazing, loving work
has been done by those who heard the voice
and kept right on working.

LIGHT IN DARK PLACES

The darkness is always present,
in our world,
in our culture,
in our minds.

It can feel heavy,
overwhelming,
depressing.

We forget that each of us have been given
the gift
of light.

If we choose, we can bring
light into dark places.

And when we dispel the darkness
for others,
ours retreats as well.

Be the Light.

WONDERING IF

Days when you wake up
a little less than inspired,
wondering if it's worth it,
regretting the past,
fearing the future,
are the days for starting with
self-compassion.

Forgive your past,
let go of the future (for a moment),
and embrace right now,

Wonder at the
overwhelming beauty of who you are,
breathe deeply,
and commit to one loving act
towards another.

Then, let the day begin.

TO YOURSELF

Every day, make a commitment.

To do the hard work.
To ask the difficult questions.
To recognize the resistance.

To care.
To be strong.
To be vulnerable.

Make this commitment
to
yourself.

Every. Single. Day.

WELCOMING THE DAY

How do you welcome the day?
"Uggh!"
"Already?"
"I want to call off today for lack of
interest."
Or
"Yes!"
"Let's go."
"Thank you."

Each response is available.
Choosing one over the other
is a habit.

Choose your greeting wisely.

IN PROCESS

If we realized everyone
(including ourselves)
is
in process,

unfinished,
unperfected,
we might be
more kind,
loving,
and
forgiving.

We might also give ourselves
more completely
in work
and
relationships,
with the understanding
that today is another day
To make mistakes,
to learn,
and grow.

It's all part of the process.

OVERWHELMING BEAUTY OF WHO YOU ARE

Just as parents don't see the growth of their
children
because they are with them every day,
we miss the overwhelming beauty
of who we are
because we see ourselves every day.

We think we are
common,
average,
ordinary.

When it comes to human beings,
there is no such thing.

The chances of your even being alive
are astronomical —
from 1 in 400 trillion to
1 in 10 to the 2,685,000th power.

So you are
a miracle,
unique,
an overwhelming beauty,
a gift,
unless you choose not to be.

Choose to own the
overwhelming beauty of who you are.

LABELS

When I was diagnosed
and given the label,
"Clinically Depressed,"
I didn't know what it meant.

I only knew how I felt.

With the diagnosis, I finally knew what I
was.

I took on the label.
I began telling myself,
"You're Clinically Depressed."
And so I was.

For 15 years.

I earned my black belt in Depression.
I nearly became a Master in
"Clinically Depressed."
I wore the label and so I became what I told
myself I was.
I didn't know what owning this label would

do
to me,
to my family,
to my life.

Be careful.
Be aware of labels others want to give you.
The life you live is your own, don't let
anyone else label you.
Choose wisely the labels you apply to
yourself.

GROWTH

Pay attention to nature and
learn of growth and death.

All of nature is either growing or dying.
Plants, animals, ponds, entire ecosystems
reflect this fact.

We forget:
We are part of nature.

If you aren't growing by
learning a new skill,
trying a different workout,
studying some new idea,
making your relationships better,
reading an interesting book,
or some other way of making progress,
then you feel like you are dying.

Without growth, you end up
wondering why you are unhappy and
unfulfilled.

Growth doesn't have to be creating a
million dollar company,
It can be walking for one more minute than
you did yesterday.

Grow.

WHAT YOU DO
EVERY DAY

If you want to know who you are,
pay attention to what you
do,
feel,
and think
every day.

These habits of
action,
emotion,
and inclination
didn't just show up one day.
You embraced them,
cultivated them and made them part of your
routine.

So if they aren't serving you,
drawing you forward,
or giving you renewed energy and life,
it's time to begin changing.

Because what you do every day is not only

who you are,
it is who you are becoming.

Decide who you want to be
and begin
doing,
thinking,
feeling
as they would—
Every. Single. Day.

STRUGGLE

If you're going to
overcome an addiction,
beat depression,
come back from injury,
build a business,
you will struggle.

If you're going to
be in better shape,
be a better lover,
be a better parent,
you will struggle.

If you're going
to seek to make progress in any area
and move from where you are
to where you want to be,
you will struggle.

So if you are in the midst of a struggle,
with a clear goal in mind,
take it as a sign you're on the right path.

Embrace the struggle.

CHANGE THE WORLD

The only way to begin to change the world:
Change yourself.

Increase your compassion capacity
(for yourself, then others).
Grow your generosity
(with both money, time and words).
Lose the unfocused anger.
Make courage a habit.
Ask for what you want and need.
Give. More. Love.

When you change, so does your world.

INTERIOR LIFE

If you want to be treated differently,
you must treat yourself differently.

FORCED LIMITS

When you give yourself
all the time in the world to fulfill a dream,
you will take all the time in the world.

We think taking our time will lead to
perfection.
Mostly, it's simple procrastination.

Our best work is more often done when we
have a constraint,
some limit on our time or resources that
focuses us,
forces us to work single-mindedly,
diligently.

So take those dreams you want to do
"someday"
and name a day, any day.
Then get to work.

DIAGNOSIS

Lost cause.
Troublemaker.
Slow learner.

ADD
ADHD

Clinically Depressed.
Chronic Anxiety.
Bi-Polar.

The diagnosis can come from
teacher,
doctor,
or neighbor.

Each one can become
a label to live up to, something to become
more of.

The troublemaker makes more trouble.
The attention deficit disorder pays less
attention.

The bi-polar becomes more manic and
more depressed.

So take care when anyone diagnoses you.

Diagnosis can be a death sentence
or
just another opinion.

UNIQUE, NOT ALONE

The facts of our uniqueness are astounding.
You and I are mathematical improbabilities.
Unique DNA.
Unique life.
Magnificent in its complexity.

Yet so often we discount ourselves as
ordinary, common, average.

Except when we are
struggling,
hurting,
or feeling ashamed.
Then, we think we are
alone,
singular,
an island.

The truth is:
Each person is unique
and
everyone struggles.

You are unique, a beautiful complexity,
but you are not alone,
unless you choose to be.

RECONSIDER

What if the
obstacles,
limitations,
brick walls,
you are facing now,
are here to
serve you,
shape you,
make you stronger?

What if all you need
to be,
and to become what you dream of,
is what you have
right
now?

What if?

WHAT LOVE ISN'T

When we focus on meeting the needs of
others
only
to get our needs met,
it's not love,
it's business.

Like the oldest profession.
A transaction.
Quid pro quo.

Unfortunately, many people think this is
what love is.
They ask,
"What have you done for me lately?"
They keep a scorecard.
And when it becomes too unbalanced,
they exit the game.

This is what love isn't.

ARMOR

Every morning,
we have a choice.
We can put on a mask,
wear battle armor,
and clank through another day.

We can hope no one notices
our fears,
our insecurities,
our emptiness.

Or we can go out,
with no mask,
and no armour,
engaging the day
with unmuted senses.

We can choose to fully
experience the richness of our life.

Or not.

END AND BEGIN

Our minds are full of things we want to do,
adventures we want to go on,
goals we want to accomplish,
feelings we want to experience.

The conflict comes when we realize
our lives are also full,
of commitments,
of priorities,
of habits.

If we are going to do something
new,
different,
fresh,
we have to stop doing something else.

What do you need to end, in order to
begin?

TROUBLING TIMES

When
troubling,
trying,
turbulent
events occur,
our tendency is to
shut down,
go inside,
and hope it will work itself out.

Or we blame everyone else,
and fail in our humanity.

Troubling times are opportunities
for us to refine
our hopes,
our dreams,
our commitments.

They are a chance for us
to get out of ourselves
and
get into the neighborhood,

to seek and do good.

They are a chance for
uncommon people
to show everyone
how to live, love and give.

GRACE

This morning,
when I opened my eyes,
the earth had made its way around the sun,
again.

Water had fallen from the skies,
nourishing the earth.

The air smelled of earth and dampness,
but was still available for inhaling.

The grass shined green.

Squirrels scurried with black walnut seeds,
again.

After all of my fret
and yesterday's furious action
checking off lists of to-do,
the earth,
the skies,
the air,
the grass,

the squirrels
didn't seem to care.

And I thought,
this
is
Grace.

SELF-LOVE

Maybe because it has the word
"self" in it,
self-love
gets equated with
self-ish,
self-important,
self-centered.

So we we teach ourselves:
If we are going to love others,
be for others,
we cannot engage in self-love.

It's self-indulgent, we tell ourselves.

Besides, we don't want anyone to catch us
preening in the mirror and saying,
"I'm good enough. I'm pretty enough,
and, darn it, people like me."
Too embarrassing.

So we hold ourselves at arms length
and call it

self-denial, self-restraint, self-control.

Maybe this should be called self-abuse.

However,
when we move toward
self-acceptance
we begin to discover a new world.

We find,
in loving ourselves,
in caring for ourselves,
a greater capacity
to love others.

We experience depths
of love we never knew existed.

And self-love transforms to true love.

THERE WILL BE PUSHBACK

If you do anything,
to move an idea forward,
to create something unique,
to express yourself,
there will be pushback.

Someone isn't going to like it.
"They" will give negative, unhelpful
feedback.
And if you listen,
the pushback
will make you
step back.

Don't.

If what you seek to push forward,
is
real,
good,
honest,
and for others well-being—

keep going.

But remember,
there will be pushback.

HOLD THE ROCK

When you work
at something
meaningful,
beautiful,
insightful,
each day can feel
like pushing a boulder
uphill.

This is good, hard, work.

But,
if all you do is
strain and push,
you will soon
expend all your energy.

Imagine running a marathon
at sprint speed
with teeth clenched.

There are times,
necessary times,

to breath deeply,
hold the rock steady,
see how far you have come,
and remember why
you're pushing in the first place.

DEDICATION

No one will be as
fired up,
excited,
or
animated
about your endeavors
as you are.

Don't let this disappoint you.

No one will ever be as
dedicated
to your life's work
as you are.

Do it anyway.

THERE IS ALWAYS AN EXCUSE

For the dream you want to pursue,
the honest work you want to do,
the art seeking to burst out of you,
there is always an excuse not to.

Which will you listen to—
the excuse or the life beckoning you?

TAKING YOUR TIME

"I went to the store today
and the clerk spent so much time with me."

"I went to the doctor
and she spent so much time with me."

"I went to the DMV and they sure took
their time."

When someone cares, we know
immediately;
they spend their time with us
carefully,
completely,
wholeheartedly.

Franchises time interactions with
customers,
seeking to make them faster and more
efficient.
It's what we expect from them, so-so
quality with speed.

Most businesses and people have defaulted
to the franchise mentality,
valuing speed over quality.

But when the person at the window takes a
moment to
recognize you,
greet you,
and treat you more than in a perfunctory
way,
immediately, the interaction becomes
something of higher quality.

It becomes a real, humane interaction,
which is what we crave.

What if you,
in your work,
your relationships,
and with yourself
began taking your time?

Be aware, if you do, people will notice.

DIAGNOSE YOURSELF

We go to doctors and therapists seeking
a name for what we are feeling.

There is immense value in consulting with
professionals
about our troubles, our struggles.
Their job is to diagnose, to label, to help us
heal.

Once we have this label, we often wear it
with pride.
"I'm ADD, ADHD, Clinically Depressed,
Bipolar, Anxiety Disorder."
Often, we feel better knowing there is a
name for our feelings.

But, what we do with that diagnosis,
the label we are given,
is critical.

Do we let it define us?
Do we become more of it?
Do we use it as a crutch, forever?

Most of who we are and how we feel is up
to us.
We can change and we do change.
So a diagnosis is rarely forever, unless we
let it be.

Ultimately, we must diagnose ourselves,
choosing what we will become
instead of living what someone said
we once were.

HABITS OF MIND

It takes time
to retrain habits of mind.

The connections and pathways
didn't pop up overnight.

They became well-worn superhighways
with regular thought, practice, and
emotions.

Habitual and unhelpful
anger,
sadness,
frustration,
overwhelm,
can be overwritten.

The interstate of the mind
can be re-routed.

But it's going to take
self-compassion,
determination

discipline,
and forgiveness.

Will you take the time to retrain
your habits of mind?

STUCK IN NEUTRAL

Where I grew up,
when the spring rains came,
the roads got mucky.
Sliding off the road
and getting stuck was a real possibility.

If you slid off the road,
you put the vehicle in neutral,
for a moment,
to take stock of the situation.

Do I need 4-wheel drive?
Do I need someone to pull me out?
Can I do this myself?

There wasn't much time spent
getting angry at the road,
or the weather,
or myself.

All I knew was:
If I stayed in neutral,
I would stay stuck.

When the rain falls in our lives,
at times of
transition,
loss,
and confusion,
it's easy to fall off the path
and get stuck.

And even easier to let this
shift us to neutral,
for more than a moment.
We get angry at
the situation,
the conditions,
and ourselves.

And then we're really stuck.

Stuck in neutral.

FEAR IS THE GROUND

Fear is the ground in which depression
grows.

We fertilize it with
self-doubt,
perfectionism,
and unrelenting self-criticism.

It grows larger,
and we sink under the shadow it casts.

We shrink it with
daily rituals
of understanding,
self-compassion,
and physicality.

Soon the ground of fear
becomes the rich soil
of love and hope
in which we grow our dreams.

YOUR BEST WORK

Every time you show
your best work,
your most vulnerable work,
your honest work,
you're going to have the desire to hide.

Don't.

Show us again.

We need to see who you really are,
so we can become who we truly are.

COMPANIONS OF COMPARISON

Jealousy and envy
are the companions of comparison.

When we compare
our situation to others,
these two show up,
bringing with them
discouragement and depression.

They are close at hand
when we
watch the
squeaky clean,
sanitized lives of friends
on Facebook, Instagram, Snapchat.

If you want to compare yourself,
compare yourself to the person
you are becoming.
Compare yourself to the person
you will be 3, 5, 10 years from now.

Ask that person,
 "How did you become wise, loving, and
joyful?"

Listen carefully for the answers.

Do those things.

Forget the companions of comparison.

DEEP BEAUTY

The deep beauty
of a person
is bound up
in the broken bits
of their lives,
not in the surface presentation
of seeming perfection.

EXPOSING OUR HUMANITY

When we attempt great things,
together,
and fail,
and try again,
we expose our humanity
in such a way
as to become connected.

When we attempt only what will work,
hide behind our carefully constructed
personas,
and fear being exposed,
deep human connection never has a chance.

So why do most of us choose the latter?

A SINGLE ACT

Your river of
stress,
worry
and fret
can be
diverted
with a single action.

Act now.

YOUR OWN TEAM

On the playground,
chosen captains
pointed to the next desired
mate for the team.
They didn't have to point at me,
I was the last one standing.
Chosen by the lack of other choices.

For years, I waited for others
to name me, to point at me,
and kept waiting.

Then I made a decision
to form my own team and
fill my roster.

I was the first selection.

In wanting so badly to be on someone else's
team,
I forgot I needed to choose myself.

Be on your own team.

CONVICTION

We convince ourselves
we are not
good enough,
smart enough,
young enough,
rich enough.

We let marketers play on those beliefs,
and never challenge what we think we
know about ourselves.

But, if we are able to convince ourselves
we are not,
then we can also convict ourselves that
we are
strong,
worthy,
able.

The hardest and best work we do
is challenging our own convictions.

FESTIVAL

Today, make time for a festival.
Go somewhere you don't usually go.
Do something you don't usually do.
Eat something you don't usually eat.
Play.

Soak
In the sights, sounds, and colors.
Celebrate the life given today.

It's a festival of you.

SILENT TEACHER

Somewhere else.
Something else.
Someone else.
So often we yearn for anything else
but
here and now.

Here and now is our teacher,
our silent, constant companion.

And yet our minds are prone
to live in the guilt of yesterday
or the anxiety of tomorrow.

And so we must
encourage,
train,
discipline ourselves
to listen for that silent teacher,
to be
here
and
now.

Or else,
somewhere else, something else, someone
else
will come
and we will miss it.

HUMAN

"Welcome to the world,"
they said,
"you're a human being."

Loved for every Ooh and Aah,
Being was a way of living.

Then, the world taught me
I would be judged by my Doing.

And Being became forgotten.

I judged myself and others
by their doing
and became
jaded,
cynical,
depressed.

In the depths,
the light of Being,
somehow,
Ignited

and began to shine.

I stumbled forward.

The journey to Being was arduous.

Doing and Being finally met,
and danced.

I've become human.

IRREPRESSIBLE
ELEGANCE

There is an irrepressible elegance
in caring about who people are.

Your
employees,
co-workers,
direct reports,
manager,
all become more
beautiful, engaged, productive,
when you engage them
first
as human beings,
not human doings.

Show you care about them,
and not just their work product
and see what develops.

UP AT NIGHT

What's keeping you up at night:
some past disappointment,
regret from paths not taken,
fear of what may happen?
or
appreciation for the day,
planning your next forward step,
anticipation for what's next?

Whatever is keeping you up at night
shows where you are living in the daylight.

(Unless it's caffeine or indigestion,
then that's another discussion.)

THE EASY WAY

The easy way means
looking for
shortcuts and workarounds.
In doing this, we try to avoid the real work
and just get the result, which often
backfires.

There is nothing wrong with seeking
simplicity and efficiency,
but others can tell when we've cut corners.

If, in your
work,
life,
relationships,
you are always seeking the easy way,
it's time to consider whether you really care
at all.

FINDING OUR WAY

When do we truly find our way?

Is it when
the path is clear,
the signposts rightly marked,
and the weather pleasant?

Or is it when
the obstacles loom large,
the way is twisted,
and we button up for storms?

We have found our way
when each is met with the same
determination.

SEEKING UNDERSTANDING

Seeking understanding doesn't mean
agreement,
it means you have listened more than you
have spoken.

Seeking understanding
opens us,
makes us vulnerable,
scares us,
but
despite what our mind may tell us,
it does not diminish us.

If we are going to do work that matters,
live lives of substance,
we must first seek to understand.

CARROTS AND STICKS

Anger does not long motivate,
nor does fear.

Dangling carrots
or
promised sticks
keep one focused
only for a short time.

To achieve your goals,
or inspire others
(for more than an
hour,
day,
week,
or a month)
the spark must be internalized.

The drive must come from within,
to do something more,
something greater,
to help others win.

YOUR WAY

When you begin
to find Your way,
make progress,
become less dis-integrated,
you will find opposition
within yourself.

Even though the body
constantly changes,
and the mind has
tens of thousands
of different thoughts a day,
they must be taught to embrace
Your new way.

When the push-back comes
(and it will)
have compassion for yourself,
but hold steady.
You are forging Your way.

THE BLACKSMITH

He didn't just show up in town one day
and think, "I'll start a fire and throw some
iron in it."

The craft was learned by
taking out the ashes,
sweeping the floor,
cleaning the tools,
watching and listening closely.

Then, there was a chance to touch iron,
to hold the tongs and the hammer,
and control the fire.

There was the ritual of slipping
on the leather apron,
thick and pitted from fire;
of pulling on the gloves,
which, in the beginning,
 were a bit too large.

As he worked the forge,
He became a forger,

copying the blacksmith's work.

Over time, he came to understand
how to create the right amount of heat,
how far to push the metal,
to create the molten colors just right for
twisting, shaping, pounding.

He didn't just show up one day,
he showed up
Every. Single. Day.
and <u>became</u> a blacksmith.

(Life is about forging yourself.
Show up every day.)

FORGING

Like a blacksmith pounding iron,
a maker of fine blades shaping steel,
you are forging
your mindset,
your art,
your resolve.

Doing work that matters
takes
heart,
strength,
and a willingness to stoke the fire,
Every. Single. Day.

WHAT MAY HAPPEN

When we worry about what may happen,
the suffering we inflict upon ourselves
is greater than the pain
of what actually occurs.

FEAR. TRUST.
OPENNESS.

Moving from fear...

to trust
ourselves,
others,
and the future
is to swim a raging river.

On the other side,
we catch our breath,
see the new landscape,
and think we have arrived.

But, there is another shore,
across an ocean.

This is the pilgrimage from
trust
to
openness.

OPENNESS

Openness is
a field of
sunflowers,
faces turned toward the sun,
accepting everything
and growing anyway.

THESE DAYS PASS

There are days,
when the sun doesn't seem to shine,
when the fire inside has cooled,
when the fog in your brain won't lift.

These days pass.

INTERJECTIONS OF AWAKENING

If I drew it up
—my life—
a thousand different times.
It would never go according to plan,
exactly.

I'd never be surprised by
anguish,
pain,
loss,
or
wonder,
joy,
grace.

So I continue to
architect my life,
but leaving space
to welcome these
interjections of awakening.

LOVE. EARLY AND OFTEN

Did you know,
fear is many times
more likely to spread
than love or good will?

Did you know,
with co-workers and acquaintances,
it takes 3 good interactions,
to overcome 1 bad one?

With family and lovers,
it takes 5!
(We are truly less forgiving to those closest
to us.)

We are often afraid to show appreciation
for a co-worker or those we are called to
lead,
but if we are going to change our world,
overcome fear,
develop dynamic workplaces,
and rich relationships,

we must apply ourselves to the project of
love,
at home,
at work,
early
and
often.

DESIGN

Your mind is constantly searching for what
is
wrong,
broken,
negative.
This may be its default setting.

If you are going to
grow,
achieve,
become,
the default must be disabled.

Become
the architect,
the engineer,
the builder,
of your
thoughts,
emotions,
and habits.

Design
your day,
your week,
your life,
with intention and purpose
or
stay in default mode.

It's up to you.

BE BORN OR DIE

Do you suppose a baby would choose to
stay in the womb?

All of her needs are met.
As far as she is concerned,
she is safe and secure.
It's warm and there is food.
Besides, this comfort is all she has ever
known.

But if she stays too long,
she will die.

We get comfortable too:
with our complaining,
with our negative focus,
with our inaction.

We say we don't like where we are,
but it's comfortable.

Unlike the baby,
we created this womb.

And,
if we stay in this comfortable space,
we will die.

We will die to
our hopes,
our dreams,
our deep desires.

We must break free from this womb
in order to be re-born,
to see the light of day,
to begin our new life.

The journey will not be easy or painless.

The choice is clear:
be born
or
die.

MANAGED

Remember, no one wants to be managed.

WHEN TRUTH SPEAKS

When truth speaks—
bone shaking
and
earth shattering

or (more likely)

soft spoken
and
subtle—

listen.

AS THE END COMES NEAR

As the end of a year,
the end of a relationship,
the end of a life,
comes near,
we look back
on mistakes made,
and lessons learned.

Some dwell on the mistakes,
assign blame and take on shame.
They worry it's too late to change.

Some focus on the battles they've won
and look forward—more to come—
forgetting the damage they've done.

Between the missteps and the battle scars
is a place to acknowledge and accept
where we have come from,
and where we are.

We leave behind the blame and shame,

and take responsibility for the pain.

And in the place of in-between,
if we are present,
the future can be seen.

HOW YOU
LOOK AT IT

Is this the end?
or
is this the beginning?

Yes.

It all depends on how you look at it.

ABOUT THE AUTHOR

Joel Morgan is a Performance and Strategic Interventionist Coach based in Richmond, Virginia. After spending 15 years clinically depressed, Joel began a journey to change his life. As he helped himself, he began to coach others to overcome and improve in all areas of life. He has coached people of all ages and backgrounds, as well as helping to forge leadership culture in nonprofit and for-profit enterprises. Joel often says his "superpower is perspective." He began writing his daily "Reflections" blog (joelmorgan.com/reflections) in 2016.

Joel is married and has two teenage boys. You can find him online at joelmorgan.com.

CPSIA information can be obtained
at www.ICGtesting.com
Printed in the USA
FSOW02n1412010717
35905FS